SNIFF, LICK & SCRATCH

Brimming with creative inspiration, how-to projects, and useful information to enrich your everyday life, Quarto Knows is a favorite destination for those pursuing their interests and passions. Visit our site and dig deeper with our books into your area of interest: Quarto Creates, Quarto Cooks, Quarto Homes, Quarto Lives, Quarto Drives, Quarto Explores, Quarto Gifts, or Quarto Kids.

© 2018 Quarto Publishing Group USA Inc.

First published in 2018 by Young Voyageur Press, an imprint of The Quarto Group, 401 Second Avenue North, Suite 310, Minneapolis, MN 55401 USA. T (612) 344-8100 F (612) 344-8692 www.QuartoKnows.com

Young Voyageur Press titles are also available at discount for retail, wholesale, promotional, and bulk purchase. For details, contact the Special Sales Manager by email at specialsales@quarto.com or by mail at The Quarto Group, Attn: Special Sales Manager, 401 Second Avenue North, Suite 310, Minneapolis, MN 55401 USA.

10 9 8 7 6 5 4 3 2 1

ISBN: 978-0-7603-6345-4

Digital edition published in 2018
eISBN: 978-0-7603-6346-1

Library of Congress Cataloging-in-Publication Data is on file.

Acquiring Editor: Dennis Pernu
Project Manager: Alyssa Lochner
Art Director: Cindy Samargia Laun

The artwork in the book is done in gouache and ink on watercolor paper.

Printed in China

MIX
Paper from responsible sources
FSC
www.fsc.org
FSC® C104723

SNIFF, LICK & SCRATCH

The SCIENCE of DISGUSTING Animal Habits

Words by Julia Garstecki   Illustrations by Chris Monroe

young
voyageur

SO, WHAT'S A HABIT?

A habit is a **behavior** people or other animals do often. In fact, they do it so often, they might not even know they do it.

To form a habit, three steps must be done over and over:

1. Perform the behavior.

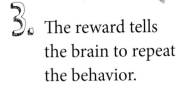

2. Get a reward!

3. The reward tells the brain to repeat the behavior.

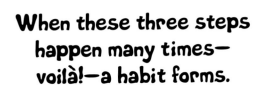

More!

Okay.

When these three steps happen many times—voilà!—a habit forms.

4

All animals have habits. Some animal habits are downright disgusting. Sometimes animals are way more disgusting than humans.

Though animal habits can seem gross, animals have reasons for these behaviors. There's even science behind them! Let's explore them and find out what animals are really doing and why.

Survival is the top reason for animal behaviors. How and what animals eat, how they clean up, and even how they cool off make the difference between life and death.

HELLO, THERE!

When humans greet each other, they wave or say, "Hello!"

Dogs, on the other hand . . .

Sometimes dogs greet other dogs by smelling their butts. It's their way of saying, "Hi. I'm Rover. I'm happy today."

See, dog butts have **anal glands** that are full of smelly liquids. By whiffing anal glands, a dog learns about the other dog's health, mood, and even what it had for breakfast.

HOW DO DOGS LEARN SO MUCH BY SMELL?

A dog's nose has about 150 million **receptors** inside it. A human nose has a measly 5 million. Scientists think a dog uses about one-third of its brain just to identify smells.

With such powerful noses, can dogs really be blamed for all that butt sniffing?

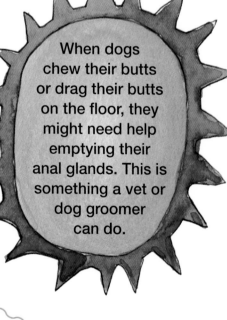

When dogs chew their butts or drag their butts on the floor, they might need help emptying their anal glands. This is something a vet or dog groomer can do.

CATS TOO?

Yes, cats smell butts too. This makes sense, because they have anal glands like dogs have.

Cats don't have the same sniffing power as dogs have, but they are better smellers than humans are. If a cat is very shy, it might sit down quickly when it meets another cat. This tells the other cat that the shy cat's butt won't be sharing any information.

Cats also greet each other with head bumps. A head bump releases **pheromones** (FAIR-uh-moans) from glands in a cat's face. Pheromones have cat information, just as anal glands do. So, if a cat is head-bumping another cat, it's not being rude. It's just curious.

Many animals have a special body part inside their mouth called Jacobson's **organ**. It helps them detect pheromones that humans can't smell. A kitten uses its Jacobson's organ to recognize its mother.

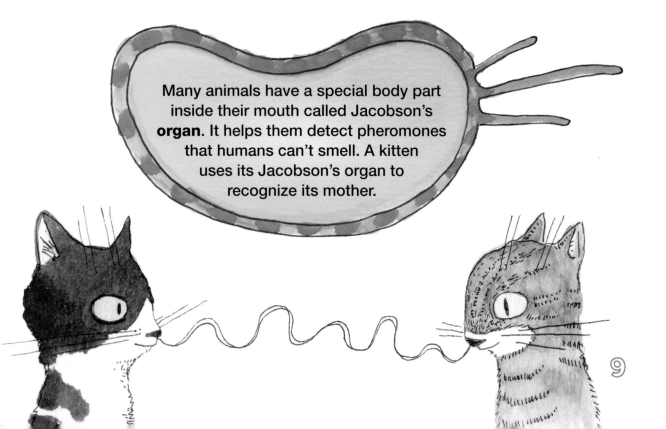

KEEP OUT!

Humans build fences to show where they live.
Of course, animals can't cut wood or pound nails.
   So how do they mark their turf?
   They leave their scent as a warning for others to
stay away. Dogs leave their scent by peeing. That's why
   you see dogs tinkling here, there, and everywhere.
   By leaving smelly pee, they're telling other dogs,
   "I own this block." Does your dog sniff
   every tree and signpost when you
take her for a walk? That's because
she's gathering information about
dogs that have been there before.

Beavers mark their
ponds and homes with a
liquid that comes out of sacs
near their butt. This liquid doesn't
smell bad to humans. In fact,
it's used to make perfumes and
sometimes even to flavor food!

Dogs are just one example. A lot of animals also leave their scent so other animals will leave them alone.

Say Bob the Deer comes across the scent of Fred the Deer. Bob wants to know if Fred is a threat or a friend. Bob finds Fred and learns Fred is a friend. After Bob and Fred become besties, Bob uses his sense of smell to find Fred and hang out with him.

And what if Bob learns that Fred is a threat? When Bob smells Fred, Bob will turn away and avoid him.

POOP POWER

Some animals have a truly gross behavior: they fling their **feces**.

Hippos toss their poop far and wide. But they don't have hands. How do they do it?

Well, they spin their tails quickly. Then they poop. The swinging tail flings the poop all over the place. It's like throwing poop at a fan.

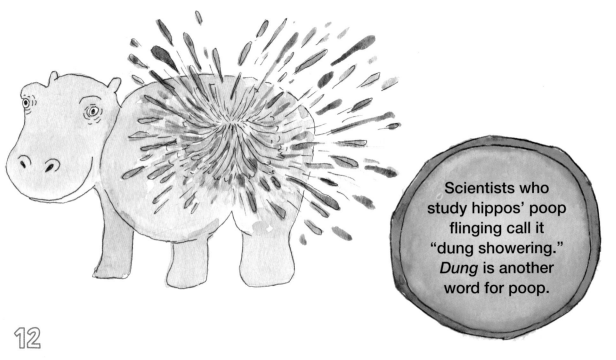

Scientists who study hippos' poop flinging call it "dung showering." *Dung* is another word for poop.

12

Hippos might do this to mark their territory. Maybe the scent helps them find their way back home. Instead of remembering to turn left at the tree like a human might, they just follow the smell of their poop.

Hippos live mostly in the water. Therefore, that is where they spray most of the poop. If you are ever in Africa and come across a hippo swimming hole, you probably shouldn't swim there.

READY, AIM, FIRE!

Hippos aren't the only animals that throw their poop. Chimpanzees, or chimps, are experts at it.

Scientists learned that chimps throw poop to express feelings or thoughts. The scientists compared poop-flinging chimps with good aim to those with bad aim. Then they studied the chimps' brains.

I'm happy.

I'm tired.

I'm bored.

In the wild, chimpanzees throw things like rocks and sticks. In zoos, they throw poop because there's usually a pile of it nearby!

14

What did the scientists discover?

Scientists learned something interesting. They found that the chimps with a better aim also had more advanced communication centers in their brains. Scientists concluded that chimps didn't learn to throw for hunting, as they once thought. They believe chimps learned to throw as a way to communicate with each other. Even though throwing poo is a way of communication for chimps, it probably isn't a good idea for us to try it!

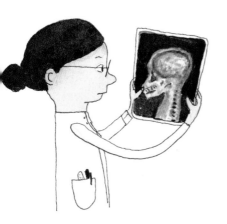

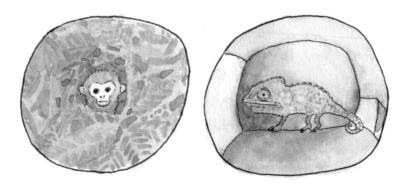

FRASS FLINGERS

Some animals get very creative to avoid **predators**. Some climb high into trees. Others change colors to help them hide. Others use their poop.

Skipper butterfly caterpillars even launch their poop! Scientists have watched this, and it's impressive. The caterpillars can send their poop, called frass, flying at 4.2 feet (1.3 meters) per second. A 6-foot-tall (1.8-meter) human with this ability could launch poop 240 feet (73 meters)!

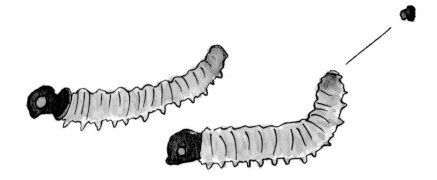

How does it work?

First, the caterpillar pumps blood into its rear end. This builds up pressure under the **anus**. When the caterpillar is ready, the frass flies! Scientists say it's like flicking a pea with your finger.

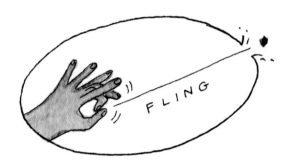

FLING

Why does the skipper butterfly caterpillar fling its frass? Because wasps are attracted to its poop. By shooting its poop far away, the caterpillar cleans out its home and keeps the wasps away too.

A skipper caterpillar makes a little leaf burrito to hide in. It produces a sticky silk that holds the leaf shut. It shoots frass outside the shelter to keep its home clean.

USEFUL POOP

Blue whales are the world's largest animals. One blue whale eats about 4 tons (3,600 kilograms) of food a day! That makes *a lot* of poop. But whale poop doesn't go to waste. It's a healthy snack for **plankton**. These tiny animals become food for larger animals. Whale poop helps balance the ocean's **food web**.

plankton

They must be really hungry . . .

The amount of food a blue whale eats in one day is equal in weight to seven grizzly bears or eight grand pianos!

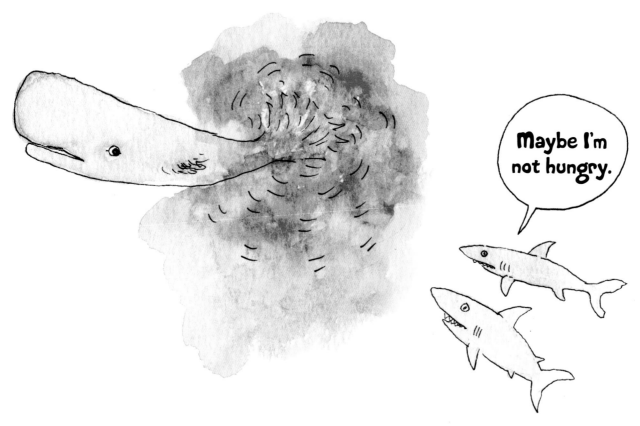

Whale poop isn't just for feeding smaller critters. Pygmy sperm whales poop to protect themselves. When they feel threatened, they poop. Then they wave the poop around with their huge fins. This makes a giant poop cloud in the water. Ideally, it grosses out the predator, who leaves to find something else to eat.

The desert tortoise does something similar. If the tortoise is threatened, it releases all its pee, which tastes awful to the predator. However, this is dangerous to the tortoise. Its pee helps it stay **hydrated** in the harsh desert.

BE MY VALENTINE?

When humans like other humans, they might buy them flowers or write a sweet note.

The male tahr shows his desire in a different way: he pees on himself. He hopes this catches the attention of a female. If she likes him, she might pee on or near the male. Pheromones in the urine send a message, like a secret note passed in class.

The tahr is a wild goat-like animal. Arabian tahrs love to climb. They can live more than 5,900 feet (1,800 meters) high in the mountains.

tahrs

The mara lives in Patagonia,
a huge and very dry area of
South America. Maras look
like rabbits with short ears and
long legs. They also use pee the
same way some humans use
wedding rings. They pee on
their partners to let other maras
know they are not available.

maras

NO POOL?
NO PROBLEM!

Summer gets hot. Humans have
several options when they need
to cool down. They can take a
swim in a pool or a run through a
sprinkler. They might have an icy
glass of lemonade. And sweat helps
humans cool off.

But a hot vulture doesn't have many choices. Like all birds, these vultures can't even sweat!

So what's an overheated vulture to do? It just pees on its legs. Like sweat on other animals, the pee cools the vulture's legs as it **evaporates**.

The pee does something else too. It kills any **bacteria** that might be clinging to the vulture's scaly legs. It seems that vultures are excellent multitaskers!

Vultures have strong stomach **acid**. It breaks down the bones of the dead animals vultures eat.

23

NO TOILET PAPER? NO PROBLEM!

Ever notice your pet doesn't wipe itself after pooping? What's up with that? Well, it doesn't have hands, of course. But there are a few other reasons too.

First, animals aren't disgusted by poop. Ever walk your dog and come across a big pile of poop? Your dog can't help but put its nose—and even its tongue—right up in the pile. Your dog is trying to see if the poop came from a familiar dog.

Second, animals don't *need* any stinkin' toilet paper. For example, cats don't mind cleaning their butts with their mouths. Sometimes they want to give you a big smooch right afterward.

Finally, animals don't really have butt cheeks. This means any clumps of clinging poop left behind will dry up and eventually fall off—or get wiped onto your carpet, if your pet is a butt dragger!

Manatees are large mammals that live in the water. If the manatee wants to float, it holds its gas in. When it wants to sink, it farts.

SCOOCH
SCOOCH
SCOOCH

Plink

CHOMP
CHOMP
CHOMP

COME AND GET IT!

All animals eat and then poop. But some animals turn right around and *eat their poop.* What gives?

This behavior is called **coprophagy** (kop-ROF-fuh-jee). It's common in animals. In fact, hamsters, elephants, beavers, pandas, and dogs all do it. Usually it's because the animal needs something in the poop, such as vitamins or healthy bacteria.

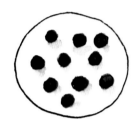

Rabbits do it too.

Rabbits make two kinds of poop. Some rabbit poop looks like dry brown pellets. Other rabbit poop is wet and comes out in wet bunches. These bunches are made when food goes through a rabbit so quickly it isn't digested all the way.

Rabbits won't eat the dry pellets, but they love the wet poop. Because it was digested so quickly, it's still full of **nutrients**. Some bunnies even eat it right from their own butts!

Did you know that some cattle in the United States are fed chicken litter?! Litter is a mixture of chicken poop, bedding, and even feathers. Yuck.

YOU GONNA EAT THAT?

Elephants eat poop too. Sometimes, though, elephants don't want their own poop. They want another animal's poop.

Elephants are beautiful, majestic creatures. Until they stick their long trunk into another elephant's butt and pull out a snack. Blech!

This behavior might help elephants add good bacteria to their **digestive systems**. Or it might just be a handy place to grab a snack.

There are only three kinds of elephants left on Earth: the African forest elephant, the African savanna elephant, and the Asian elephant. Elephants can't jump or trot, but they can swim, using their trunk as a snorkel.

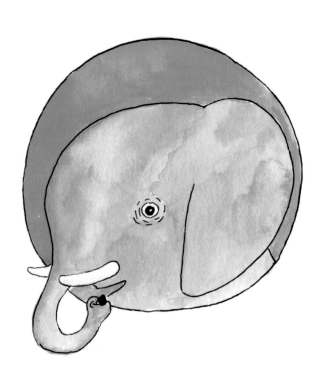

There are other animals that find elephant poop useful too: humans!

Elephants in the Golden Triangle area of Thailand are fed coffee beans. Digestive juices in their guts break down the beans and bring out their sweetness. When the elephants poop, workers pick the beans out of the poop. Then they wash the beans and roast them. People will pay up to five hundred dollars a pound for these coffee beans!

Don't you wonder who tried this first?

BEHOLD, THE DUNG BEETLE

Eating poop seems pretty icky to humans, even when we know the reasons. But some animals take it a step further. They work, live, *and* play in poop.

Dung beetles live on every continent except Antarctica. And you might find them anywhere there's animal dung. The dung beetle didn't get its name from living in grassy meadows!

Dung beetles roll pieces of poop into balls. Then the beetles save the balls for snacks or as places to lay their eggs. Some dung beetles even live in piles of dung they make.

Dung beetles are choosy about their poop. They prefer the dung of plant-eating animals called **herbivores**. Herbivores don't digest their food very well. That means they leave more nutrients behind in their poop.

Dung beetles are serious recyclers. They make sure nothing is wasted—not even poop from other animals!

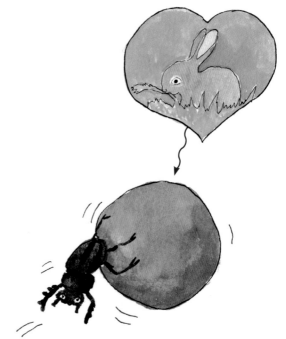

Scientists watched a dung beetle roll a poop ball 1,141 times its body weight. That would be like a 150-pound (68-kilogram) person rolling a poop ball weighing 160,000 pounds (72,575 kilograms)!

HOME SWEET HOME

BARF EATERS

What's your favorite meal? Did you say barfed-up seeds and bugs? You must be a bird!

Regurgitation is common among birds. This is when a bird throws up small bits of food and feeds them to another bird. When a mother bird is protecting her eggs, she can't leave her nest. A predator could steal her eggs for a delicious breakfast. So the male flies out into the world and gathers food. But he can't fly with grocery bags on his wings. And birds don't have pockets. If he can't carry the food with his feet, what's a father to do?

When a male bird tries to attract a female, he'll regurgitate for her. It shows he can provide for her. If he's lucky, she is impressed!

The answer is that he eats until he can't eat anymore. Then he flies back to the nest and barfs up his dinner for the mother bird to eat. When the babies hatch, she will feed them the same way. Yum!

LEFTOVERS

It turns out lots of birds have habits we humans might think are nasty. Birds such as owls, hawks, and eagles are known as birds of **prey**. They hunt small animals for their food, such as mice, rabbits, smaller birds, fish, and even snakes. Often, birds of prey gulp down their victims whole. But they can't digest their prey's bones, teeth, hair, or feathers.

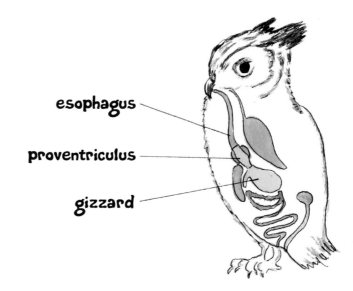

esophagus

proventriculus

gizzard

These undigested leftovers collect in the bird's **gizzard**. There, they are mashed up into a tight bundle called a pellet.

Here's where it gets a little gross. The bird of prey barfs up the pellet. You might find a bird pellet in the forest. You can **dissect** it and learn what the bird had for lunch. Maybe you've even done this in science class.

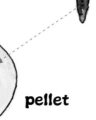

pellet

Owls are great hunters. One reason for this is that their ears let them hear the tiniest prey from 60 feet (18 meters) away!

TEAR JERKERS

Ever think about poking somebody in the eye and drinking their tears? I didn't think so. But this is exactly what butterflies and bees do.

This is called *lachryphagy* (lak-RIF-uh-jee). It means "tear-feeding." The victims are usually turtles and crocodiles.

The eye poking causes tears to flow. Then the insect drinks up the tears. This might seem strange. But bees and butterflies do it for a reason. See, tears have nutrients the insects need. Lachryphagy doesn't seem to harm the turtles or crocs, though they might find it a little annoying . . .

One scientist let more than two hundred bees drink from his eyes! The bees used their legs to hold on to his eyelashes. Then they slurped up his tears. They didn't sting him, but his eyes itched for a few days.

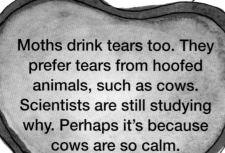

Moths drink tears too. They prefer tears from hoofed animals, such as cows. Scientists are still studying why. Perhaps it's because cows are so calm.

Animal Hygiene

It's easy for humans to get clean. We have bathtubs and showers. We have all kinds of soaps and shampoos too. But it's important for animals to stay clean, just as it is for humans.

Dirty feathers make it hard for birds to fly and escape hungry predators. Other animals might attract bugs if they're too smelly. And if that's not bad enough, filth attracts **parasites**. If animals don't groom themselves (or sometimes each other), parasites make the animals sick.

Animals have many ways of keeping clean. Some of these methods might seem disgusting to us, but they're just how the animals clean up.

And when it comes to food, most animals don't care about cleanliness. Humans, macaques, and some pigs are the only animals known to wash their food.

39

BATH TIME!

Any interest in **saliva** soap? Cat owners know that their pet cats are expert bathers. So are big cats, such as lions and tigers. They spend about half their day grooming themselves.

If we humans smell bad, we might get embarrassed. But for many animals, staying clean means staying alive. If a big cat's prey smells the cat, the prey gets scared off and the cat goes hungry. Likewise, if the prey is stinky, and the big cat gets a whiff, the prey had better look out. The best way to not get eaten? Don't be smelly.

How does all this cat grooming work? Well, lions, tigers, leopards, and even pet cats have rough tongues that help them lick bugs and dirt from their fur. Think of their tongues as hairbrushes with tiny bristles. Cats spend a lot of time using their tongues to remove stuff like smelly old food from their paws and whiskers.

And cats can reach pretty much anywhere on their bodies. Often, mother lions lick their babies clean until the cubs are old enough to do it themselves. The next time your mom asks you to shower, just be glad you're not a cat!

Sometimes a cat swallows too much hair from all its grooming. Then, look out! It'll barf up a hairball.

Hands off, sis!

PRIMPING PRIMATES

If your brother or sister picked at your skin, you would probably make them stop. But **primates** often pick at each other. They aren't trying to annoy each other like pesky siblings. All that poking and pinching serves a purpose. They're grooming each other, like when people brush their hair.

Scientists who study primates think this behavior helps primates learn to cooperate. Mother baboons and monkeys groom their babies. The babies practice grooming on their moms. They learn to pick out dirt, insects, and parasites, and smooth tangled fur.

So, would you rather take a shower or ask your little brother to pick at you?

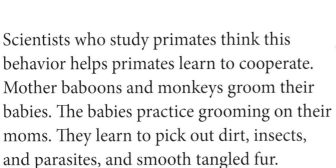

In South Africa, baboons sometimes sneak into houses and steal food from human families.

UNDERWATER SPA

Primates aren't the only animals that offer cleaning services to other animals. The scarlet skunk cleaner shrimp provides wonderful grooming to fish and eels. The eel or fish opens its mouth wide, and the shrimp swims inside. It might even swim down the fish's throat. The shrimp picks and eats bacteria, dead **cells**, and parasites.

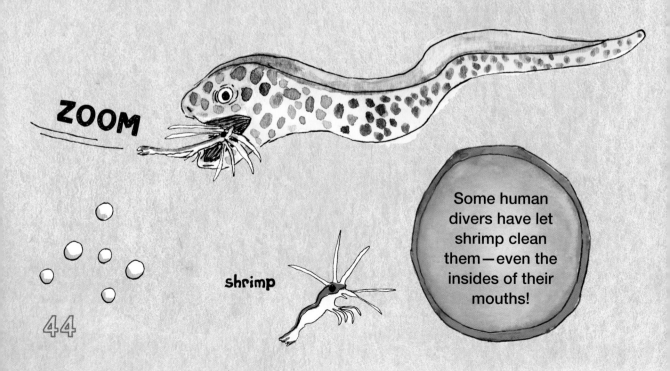

ZOOM

shrimp

Some human divers have let shrimp clean them—even the insides of their mouths!

This is a **symbiotic** (sim-bee-AH-tic) relationship. It means both animals get something out of it. The fish or eel gets a good cleaning. The shrimp gets a snack! There are many examples of symbiotic relationships in the animal world.

OPEN WIDE

How often do you brush your teeth? Not brushing could become a bad habit.

But what about other animals? When's the last time your pet goldfish brushed its teeth? Never?

Well, some animals *do* take care of their teeth. For example, elephants take good care of their tusks, which are basically long teeth. They rub their tusks against trees. They dig holes with them. The digging might look like fun, but it keeps the tusks strong.

46

Some teeth never stop growing. Think about bunnies and guinea pigs. (Who doesn't like to do that?) They must keep chewing, or their teeth will grow out of control. When you see them munching a stick really fast, they are taking care of their teeth.

Do you have a pet guinea pig? It's a good idea to put a wood block in its cage. This gives the guinea pig something to chew on and help keep its teeth from getting too long. Plenty of hay or grass helps too.

47

NOSE-PICKING ANIMALS

Humans aren't the only animals that pick their boogers! Lots of animals get in on that action. Gorillas pick their noses the same way people do. Then they eat it up! Mother gorillas help their babies with stuffy noses. Mom clamps her mouth over the baby's nose and sucks out the snot, just like a vacuum cleaner.

Capuchin monkeys use sticks to yank out a booger—or ten. They also use sticks to tickle their noses and make them sneeze. Then the rest of the snot just flies out!

capuchin monkey

AH-CHOO

But what if an animal doesn't have fingers for nose picking? What can it do?

Luckily for the giraffe, its tongue is about 20 inches (51 centimeters) long. Sometimes a giraffe blows its nose real hard and then cleans up the mess with its tongue. Other times it just slips its long tongue right up its nose and cleans it out.

When the giraffe's nose is booger-free, it's time for an ear cleaning.

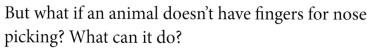

A giraffe's neck can be more than 6 feet (1.8 meters) long! Giraffes' long necks and legs make them the tallest animals in the world.

SELF-DEFENSE

Sometimes the animal kingdom is dangerous. A lot of animals develop **defense mechanisms** that help them survive. While some of these might seem disgusting to humans, they're also pretty cool.

For example, some animals squirt stuff out of their bodies. Take the horned lizard, for example. It blends in with the desert where it lives. But if a wolf or other predator smells it, the horned lizard has a backup defense: it floods its eyes with blood! Then it squirts the red liquid. While the predator is freaking out about being squirted with blood, the horned lizard scurries away!

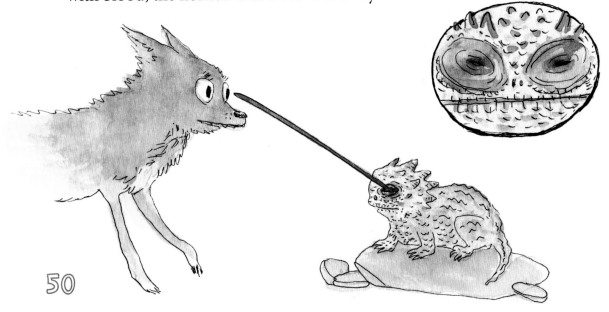

Bombardier beetles also spray attackers. The beetle has two sacs inside its body. Each sac contains a different liquid. When the beetle is scared, the liquids mix. Then the beetle shoots them at the attacker with a loud *pop*! The liquid is the same temperature as boiling water! It bothers the attacker's eyes and lungs.

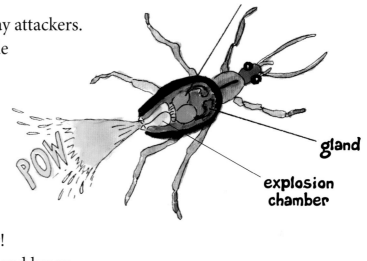

sac

gland

explosion chamber

POW

Scientists once watched a frog eat a bombardier beetle. Moments later, the frog barfed up the beetle, which walked away unharmed.

sea
cucumber

INSIDE OUT

Some defense mechanisms have a high gross factor. The sea cucumber oozes its guts out its anus. This awesome skill is called *self-evisceration* (self ih-viss-uh-RAY-shun).

Some sea cucumbers even have an extra-special weapon: poisonous **intestines**. The sea cucumber poops out its guts and gets away. Later, it grows back its guts.

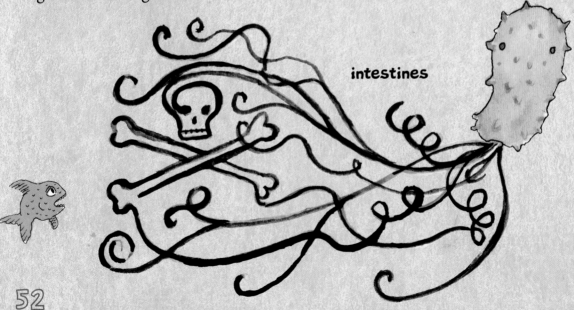

intestines

hagfish

The hagfish is another ocean dweller with a gross self-defense tactic. When this eel-like fish gets in a dangerous situation, it squirts a thick slime from glands all along its sides. The slime mixes with water and quickly expands. The predator gets so tangled up and smothered in the slime that the hagfish has time to get away.

Hagfish feed on dead animals on the ocean floor. They tunnel through the dead animals and eat them from the inside out.

WHAT'S THAT SMELL?

Squirting slime is awesome, but sometimes nasty smells do the job just as well.

Skunks are famous for their nasty spray. They have two glands near their anus. When an attacker gets too close, they flex muscles back there. The result? A spray that can be smelled a mile away. If the spray hits the predator in the eye, it can be blinded for a little while.

If you or your pet gets sprayed by a skunk, some people might suggest using tomato juice to get rid of the smell. But this doesn't really work. In many cases, you just have to wait a long time for the smell to go away. A. Very. Long. Time.

millipede

A millipede is an insect with many, many, many legs all along its sides. Its name means "thousand feet," but no millipede really has that many feet.

Millipedes are a lot smaller than skunks. But they still get pretty stinky. Some millipedes release **chemicals** through tiny holes in their bodies that drive away predators.

Other animals find the millipede's chemicals useful. Scientists have watched monkeys rub millipedes on their bodies. The monkeys learned that the millipede chemicals keep mosquitoes away!

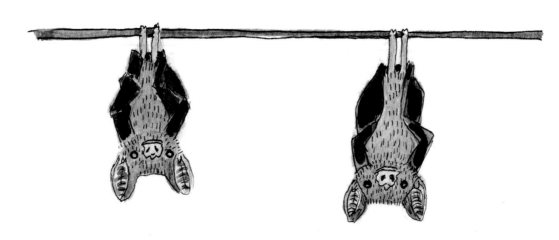

SPACE INVADERS

Some animal behavior isn't disgusting, it's just creepy.

Vampire bats live in Mexico, Central America, and South America. They have *very* sharp teeth. Their teeth are so sharp, victims rarely even feel them pierce their skin. That's a good thing for the bats. Vampire bats like to choose the same victim over and over. Scientists think vampire bats recognize the same victim by how it breathes.

You shouldn't worry about vampire bats. They prefer to suck blood from animals such as cattle, horses, and chickens.

Another animal with a creepy habit is the brown tree snake. It lives in Australia and on islands in the Pacific Ocean. It seems to bite sleeping children more than adults. Experts aren't sure why. It might be because there's something yummy about sleeping children. Or maybe small children are just easier victims. Either way, it's pretty creepy!

The bedbug is another creepy home invader. Bedbugs are tiny. They dine on human blood when their victim is asleep at night.

So which animal do you think is the most disgusting?

It's hard to say. Besides, who are we to talk? Humans can be pretty gross too!
Even if we have a tissue, we sometimes use our fingers for booger control.
At least we don't eat poop or someone else's chewed-up food!

It's important to remember that even though some animal habits seem gross, they are survival skills. For example, picking bugs off their babies will keep a group of monkeys healthy. Smelling butts helps dogs and cats know if another animal is dangerous.

So the next time you see an animal do something yucky, think about why it's doing this. Then be glad you have a bathtub to wash in and a plate to eat from!

GLOSSARY

acid—a strong chemical substance. Some acids help humans and other animals digest their foods.

anal glands—sacs near an animal's anus that produce smelly fluids that animals use to identify one another

anus—the opening at the end of the large intestine through which poop exits the body

bacteria—tiny single-cell bodies that live on every part of the earth and inside most animals. Some bacteria are harmful, while others are helpful for things like digestion.

behavior—the usual actions of an animal

cells—tiny units of life that include a center called a *nucleus* and an outer wall called a *membrane*. Both plants and animals have cells.

chemicals—very basic, tiny substances that combine to make other substances

coprophagy—the behavior of eating poop

defense mechanisms—actions animals take to protect themselves. Often an animal doesn't even realize it's taking action.

digestive system—a group of organs that helps an animal turn eaten food into energy

dissect—to cut open and examine

evaporates—turns from liquid to gas

feces—poop, also known as dung

food web—a community's food sources that relate to and affect one another

gizzard—a muscular organ that helps a bird digest its food

hydrated—having the amount of water needed in one's body to be healthy

herbivores—animals that eat only plants

intestines—long, coiled tubes between the stomach and anus that help digest food

nutrients—things in food that help animals or plants grow and survive

organ—a part of a plant or animal that does a specific job. The brain, heart, and stomach are examples of organs.

parasites—living things that survive by living in or on other living things

pheromones—chemicals released by an animal to trigger a response from the same kind of animal

plankton—very tiny plants and animals that float in ocean water and are an important food source for whales

predators—animals that eat other animals

prey—an animal that is a food source for another animal

primates—a classification of mammals that includes monkeys, apes, and humans

receptors—nerve endings that receive information

regurgitation—the act of throwing up

saliva—a liquid produced in the mouth to help swallow and digest food

symbiotic—describes a relationship that benefits both members

INDEX